Automatic mapping of ontology into relational database

Humaira Afzal

Automatic mapping of ontology into relational database

LAP LAMBERT Academic Publishing

Impressum / Imprint
Bibliografische Information der Deutschen Nationalbibliothek: Die Deutsche Nationalbibliothek verzeichnet diese Publikation in der Deutschen Nationalbibliografie; detaillierte bibliografische Daten sind im Internet über http://dnb.d-nb.de abrufbar.
Alle in diesem Buch genannten Marken und Produktnamen unterliegen warenzeichen-, marken- oder patentrechtlichem Schutz bzw. sind Warenzeichen oder eingetragene Warenzeichen der jeweiligen Inhaber. Die Wiedergabe von Marken, Produktnamen, Gebrauchsnamen, Handelsnamen, Warenbezeichnungen u.s.w. in diesem Werk berechtigt auch ohne besondere Kennzeichnung nicht zu der Annahme, dass solche Namen im Sinne der Warenzeichen- und Markenschutzgesetzgebung als frei zu betrachten wären und daher von jedermann benutzt werden dürften.

Bibliographic information published by the Deutsche Nationalbibliothek: The Deutsche Nationalbibliothek lists this publication in the Deutsche Nationalbibliografie; detailed bibliographic data are available in the Internet at http://dnb.d-nb.de.
Any brand names and product names mentioned in this book are subject to trademark, brand or patent protection and are trademarks or registered trademarks of their respective holders. The use of brand names, product names, common names, trade names, product descriptions etc. even without a particular marking in this work is in no way to be construed to mean that such names may be regarded as unrestricted in respect of trademark and brand protection legislation and could thus be used by anyone.

Coverbild / Cover image: www.ingimage.com

Verlag / Publisher:
LAP LAMBERT Academic Publishing
ist ein Imprint der / is a trademark of
OmniScriptum GmbH & Co. KG
Heinrich-Böcking-Str. 6-8, 66121 Saarbrücken, Deutschland / Germany
Email: info@lap-publishing.com

Herstellung: siehe letzte Seite /
Printed at: see last page
ISBN: 978-3-659-76367-0

Zugl. / Approved by: Comsats University Lahore, 2013

ABSTRACT

Automatic Mapping of Ontology to Relational Database Schema

The semantic web is gaining significance day by day. There must be an efficient and automatic approach to transform all ontology constructs in to relational database so that it can be queried easily. The mapping of ontology data in to relational data base ease operations like data searching and retrieval. Research work has been done on transformation of RDF/OWL concepts into relational database. But there exist problems in direct transformation and mapping of ontology information to relational database. Some approaches claim that their method of transformation is fully automatic but the transformation process is incomplete and they miss important OWL constructs. The purpose of this thesis is to propose a new fully-automatic and lossless approach for transformation of ontology into relational database format. In this thesis, we also present our experience of using this new approach on different ontologies to illustrate/showcase how ontology can be transformed into Relational database format.

TABLE OF CONTENTS

LIST OF FIGURES

LIST OF TABLES

LIST OF ABBREVIATIONS

FK   Foreign Key
PK   Primary Key
RDB   Relational Data Base
OWL   Web Ontology Language

Chapter 1
Introduction

World Wide Web is an interesting paradigm for learning. The websites we explore every day, use natural languages and images to present information in understandable way. As we all know computers do not understand the information because they cannot see or analyze relationships and make important decisions. So to extract meaning-full information becomes a difficult task. The Web just gives 20-25% relevant results. To solve these problems, information should be expressed in machine-targeted language. This calls for a new approach "Semantic Web".

The term "Semantic Web" was originated by Tim Berners-Lee, inventor of the WWW, URIs, HTTP, and HTML.

"Semantic Web represents a set of semantically and formally interlinked data units - thereby creating a Semantic Web inside the Web" [Berners-Lee, RM].

The Semantic Web approach helps computers to understand and use the Web. The main idea behind Semantic Web is very simple; add metadata to web pages that can make the current Web machine readable. This won't make computers self-aware, but it will provide tools to search interpret and exchange information [1].

There exist two major differences between Web and Semantic Web

(1) In Semantic Web, information is expressed in machine-targeted language, whereas the Web contains information targeted for human consumption, expressed in a wide range of natural languages [2].
(2) The Semantic Web presents semantically interconnected data, whereas in Web information is informally interconnected [2].

The Semantic Web modifies the Web data in such a way that it is understandable to computers. It enables machines and applications to perform searching, and consolidation for information without any human intervention. Ontology has been widely used in Semantic Web and other related fields. The purpose of ontology is to capture knowledge of related fields. Ontology is used to understand the structure of information and reuse of domain knowledge [2].

2

The Semantic Web is gaining significance day by day. There are different techniques for storing ontology. We can store ontology in flat files. But this technique does not provide scalability, query and other functionalities that database system can provide. Ontology management system can store ontology in ontology repositories. But query facility in ontology management system is not as developed as that of relational database system. The relational database system has many advantages over ontology management system like performance, robustness, maturity, reliability and availability [2].

Large amount of Web data is stored in relational format. So when ontology is stored in relational database, it can interoperate with large amount of existing data in relational format. Relational database gives scalability to the queries and reasoning on knowledge provided by ontology. Efficient reasoning and querying on ontology will make Semantic Web more useful.

Mapping of ontology in relational database facilitates operations like searching and retrieval. Mostly research work has been done on direct transformation of relational database to RDF/OWL concepts and description. But there exist problems in direct transformation and mapping of ontology concepts to relational database. So It is required to develop a tool from OWL ontology to relational database that is fully-automatic and can solve problems.

1.1   Why We Need OWL to RDB Transformation

Mostly Web data is stored in relational format. So when ontology is stored in relational database it can interoperate with large amount of existing data in relational format. Relational database gives scalability to the queries and reasoning on knowledge provided by ontology. Efficient reasoning and querying on ontology will make Semantic Web more useful.

Previous transformation approaches from OWL ontology to relational database, face certain problems i.e.

-   Loss of structure and data
-   Perform initial mappings only
-   Most of transformation methods are semi-automatic and need human intervention.

3

There is need to develop a tool that can fully automatically transform ontology to relation database without any human intervention. Later this tool could be used in different projects involved in data integration.

1.2 Challenges

Mapping of Ontology to Relational database is an important issue in the development of Semantic Web. Previous transformation approaches from OWL ontology to relational database, face certain problems i.e. loss of structure, loss of data, manual and semi-automatic. They are limited and in many cases they just perform initial mappings i.e. tables to classes and columns to properties.

Most of transformation methods are semi-automatic and need human intervention. Some approaches claim that their method of transformation is fully automatic but the transformation process is incomplete and they miss important OWL constructs. Existing tools, plug-ins and utilities are not easily accessible and need improvement. So there is need to develop a transformation tool from OWL ontology to relational database that is fully-automatic and can solve above mentioned problems.

1.3 Contributions

Our study mainly focuses on the following points.

The technological advancement in Semantic Web requires improvement in Semantic knowledge Models. Mostly research work done on direct transformation of relational database to RDF/OWL concepts and description. But problem exists in direct transformation and mapping of ontology concepts to relational database. So our research focus is to develop a tool from OWL ontology to relational database that is fully-automatic and can solve above mentioned problems.

1. The importance of relational database in Semantic Web field is evident, so ontology to relational database mapping can be used in different applications or fields. Ontology can interoperate with a large amount of data that has already been stored in relational databases.

4

2. Through mapping, we can share information. Querying the system will be more advance, robust and optimized. A common goal is the consolidation of distributive information, in the form of common vocabulary.

3. The building blocks in Web engineering are ontology and relational database. And large amount of Web data is stored in relational format. If relational schema and ontology were building independently, it complicates things. There are some parts of database which are not included in Ontology. The majority of existing applications need integration among these systems. Through this mapping ontological data can be access from existing Relational database applications.

1.4 Organization of Thesis

This thesis is divided into six chapters starting from the brief introduction about Semantic Web technologies and mapping of ontology into relational database format (Chapter 1) which further leads to the mapping of ontology into relational format approach (Chapter 2) from literature review. Chapter 3 explains our research approach and system architecture .Chapter 4 explains implementation details. Then we present a detail analysis and evaluation of proposed system with the help of case study (Chapter five). Finally Chapter 6 concludes our research work with some future directions.

Chapter 2

Related Work

In this chapter, we will discuss important concepts of Semantic Web, ontologies and their types, relational database, its importance, Jena API, SQL server and languages of Semantic Web. Then we describe the existing methods and approaches for ontology to relational database format. At the end of the chapter, we describe the drawbacks and comparison of existing techniques.

2.1   Semantic Web

The Web sites we explore every day use natural languages and images to present information in understandable way. Computers do not understand the information because they cannot see or analyze relationships and make important decisions [3]. The main reason behind this issue is that the Web data is not organized properly and not in machine readable form.

The Semantic Web approach helps computers to understand information and use the Web. The main idea behind Semantic Web is very simple; add metadata to Web pages that can make the current Web, machine readable. This provides machines to search interpret and exchange information [3].

Semantic Web is the modification of current Web from human readable form to machine process able form. It provides advanced functionality and more Web applications. Due to Semantic Web, computers will be able to search, process, integrate and present the contents in a better, meaningful and intelligent manner.

The Semantic Web is not a separate unit from the World Wide Web. It is extension of Web which adds new data to existing Web documents. The extension of Web documents enable the Web to be processed automatically by machines. For this task RDF (Resource Description Framework) is used to change basic Web data into structured data.

The basic aim of Semantic Web is to modify the Web data in such a way that it is understandable to computers, enable machines and applications to perform searching, and consolidation for information without any human intervention.

The appearance of Semantic Web gives new pattern of computing in different research areas like data integration where data is distributed and heterogeneous. Due to Semantic Web computers will be able to present the contents in a better, meaningful and intelligent manner. The purpose of Semantic Web is the application of advanced systems for management of knowledge and information.

2.2. Ontology

Ontology is defined as

"Ontology is an explicit specification of conceptualization."- Gruber '91

It improves the accuracy and efficiency of Web search. At present, the most important ontology language is OWL. OWL is a description language for describing properties, classes, relations between classes, cardinality, equality, characteristics of properties (e.g. symmetry), and enumerated classes[1].

Ontology has been widely used in Semantic Web and other related fields. The purpose of ontology is to capture knowledge of related fields. Ontology is used to understand the structure of information and reuse of domain knowledge [1].

2.2.1. Main Components of Ontology

Ontology contains a list of terms, and relationship between these terms. These terms are used to explain important concepts of the domain.

Ontology includes information such as:

- Classes and subclasses
- Properties
- Value Restrictions
- Disjoint statements
- Individuals

2.2.1.1 Classes

Classes represent the basic concepts of domain ontology and they are the building block of different classification trees.

2.2.1.2 Individuals

Individuals also known as instances are basic unit of ontology. It can be referred as 'instances of classes'. These are the formal part of ontology and describe the entities of interest.

2.2.1.3 Properties

Property describes various characteristics of class. They link two individuals and present relationship. Properties are divided in two types.

1. Object type properties

    These are relationships between two individuals. Each object property may have its corresponding inverse property.

2. Data type properties

    They describe relationships between individuals and data values (XML schema data type value).

2.2.2 Kinds of Ontologies

There are two main types of ontologies i.e. domain ontologies and upper ontologies. Domain ontologies: They use to model a specific and precise domain, which represents unit of the world e.g. banking system.

Upper ontologies: It is also known as top level or foundation ontology. It describes very common concepts. They use to model general objects that are relevant to many domain ontologies.

2.3   Semantic Web Languages

Today, the most valuable languages for ontology are as follows:

• RDF is a data model and framework for describing objects ("Web resources") and relations between them. It also provides a simple semantics for these objects, and these can be written in XML syntax.

• RDF Schema is an extended form of RDF. It is also known as vocabulary description language and describes classes and properties of RDF resources.

• OWL means Web ontology language. It is use for processing Web information. It has richer vocabulary for illustrating all ontology concepts and their relationships [3].

2.4 Resource Description Framework (RDF)

The Resource Description Framework (RDF) is accepted structure to illustrate any Web resource. It is used to explain and exchange meta data (data about Web resources). RDF description may contain the authors of specific resource, updating or creation date, the sitemap, information about content, key words (for search engine), and so forth. It provides machine understandable semantics that leads to accuracy in resource searching. It is an extension of Extensible Markup Language, and developed under the guidance of the World Wide Consortium.

In RDF, every statement or expression is a collection of triplets. And every triplet defines subject, object and predicate as shown in figure 2.1. The arc direction is important and it always points towards object. This triplet shows some relationship between subject and object, indicated by predicate.

Figure 2.1 Triplets in RDF

The Hypertext Markup Language (HTML) was already providing some amount of metadata for Web site resources. For example, in any Web page development, we can add HTML statements that contain some key words. These key words explain the content of this definition, and further used by search engines for indexing [4].

But RDF encourages the provision and maintenance of metadata about internet resources. Because RDF supports standard syntax for defining and querying data, so software that

10

utilizes metadata will be easier and faster to produce, and allow applications to exchange information more easily.

2.5   RDFS

RDFS- RDF is vocabulary description language. RDFS can be used to describe ontology. It is a simple data type model for RDF. Through RDFS, we can describe groups of resources and the relationship among them. The basic purpose of RDF schema is to define classes and their relationship (sub classes), express properties and relate them with classes. It facilitates interpretation of data and improves searching [4].

2.6   OWL

OWL provides three sub languages used for specific purpose. These are OWL-Lite, OWL-DL and OWL Full. The less expressive Sub-language is OWL-Lite and OWL-Full is considered as high expressive sub-language.

2.6.1 OWL-Lite

OWL-Lite is the simplest and easy sub-language. It is used in conditions where only a simple constraints and simple classification hierarchy is required.

2.6.2 OWL-DL

OWL-DL is more expressive as compared to OWL-Lite while retaining computational completeness. OWL-DL and OWL-Lite are based on Description Logics. In OWL-DL all OWL language concepts are included but it can be used under some conditions.

2.6.3 OWL-Full

OWL-Full is the most expressive language. It supports the users who want maximum syntactic freedom and expressiveness of RDF with no computational assurance

2.7   Database

The concept of a relational database was first established in 1969 by Edgar Frank Codd [5].

There are several advantages of a relational database over any other system

- Solve data duplication
- It avoids inconsistent records
- Easier to change data
- Easier to change data format
- Data can be added and removed easily
- Easier to maintain security
- Relational database gives scalability to the queries and reasoning on knowledge provided by ontology [6].

The Semantic Web data model has connection with relational databases model.

2.8 Existing approaches

Technological advancement in Semantic Web requires improvement in Semantic knowledge models. When discussing Ontology to relational database mapping, we notice that there are many approaches for OWL to relational database and inverse mapping. But face certain problems i.e. loss of structure, loss of data, manual and semi-automatic. They are limited and in many cases they just perform initial mappings i.e. tables to classes and columns to properties.

Our research community needs to develop a tool from OWL ontology to relational database that is fully-automatic and can handle wider range of OWL constructs. This type of tool is required so that people can easily convert their ontology to the database. This tool will also help them in quick data searching and retrieval.

Previous ontology to relational database transformation approaches e.g. OWL to ER and ER to OWL use conceptual graphs and they perform step-wise transformations where first step is to transform the OWL ontology to ER and second step is to transform ER to relational database. Direct transformation is not possible in this case and its time consuming approach. [3]. "Oracle Semantic data storage" approach is also used but most OWL constructs are missing [10].

Gali *et al.* introduces a set of techniques for lossless mapping of OWL Ontology to relational database. In previous approaches, special purpose database and an object oriented database system is used to store and retrieve ontological information. XML mapping approaches like edge, attribute, universal, normalized and basic in-lining have been proposed. Brief description of these approaches is given below.

Edge Approach: Store all the attributes information (object identities, name, and flag) in a single table called Edge table.

Attribute approach: Attributes with the same name are grouped into one table.

Universal approach: Store all attributes with separate columns for each attribute present in XML document.

Normalized universal approach: Introduces separate overflow tables for multi valued attributes.

Basic In lining Approach: It maps the XML DTD into relations.

Above approaches are not fully applicable while transforming OWL to relational database [13].

Gali *et al.* use relational database to map ontology data. Their mapping system consists of three parts i.e. *Ontology modeler, Document manager and Ontology reasoner.*

Ontology Modeler: It takes OWL documents and creates an ontology model; few constraints are considered and recorded during parsing.

Document Manager: It involves processing and handling of OWL documents and use Jena for importing OWL documents.

Ontology Reasoner: It provides method for listing, getting and setting that RDF type of sources.

They developed the algorithm "OWL2DB" to map OWL document into relational table. The major steps are parsing the OWL file for root classes. They determine the depth of descendants through iteration and keep track of the depth of the subclasses from root. If the depth of graph is three then relational table is created for all the sub-classes. This step is repeated until all the information like table-names and column-names is collected. Next step is to collect the values of instances to populate the database. Graph is parsed

13

again to collect the values stored in a data structure. A database connection is established and all the tables are created and values are inserted.

To evaluate the performance of system, experiments on two OWL files are presented. These files are parsed and separate relations are created for all children nodes at different depths. The nodes are in-lined. After every mapping queries are executed and optimal performance is decided.

Gali *et al.* propose an approach to map OWL documents into relational tables without any human intervention. They have also proposed few mapping rules for transformation. But the transformation is incomplete and it only saves class instances in relational format. As the Semantic Web is gaining importance there is a need of an efficient approach to map all ontology information so that it can be efficiently queried later [13].

To solve problems in OWL to database transformation, Irina *et.al* proposes a new transformation approach based on "mapping rules" and implements their approach in a utility call "QUALEG DB". The rules proposed for QUALEG DB are applicable to any ontology (because specified on model level), and explains how to transform OWL constructs to relational database.

"QUALEG DB" can automatically transform OWL ontology to relational database. The engine parses an OWL file and generates SQL script. It also performs consistency and error checks. The drawback of this approach is that some of OWL constructs are lost during transformation like sub-properties. Another problem is that few if the OWL constructs are not considered e.g. types of property restrictions [2].

Ernestas *et al.* proposes an algorithm for transformation of ontology to relational database in 2006. Their algorithm is based on OWL2DB approach. The algorithm is tested on ontology example taken from product configuration domain. Their approach only covers part of OWL DL syntax. So there is a need to represent more advanced OWL features [14].

Ernestas *et al.* propose some principles and algorithm for automatic transformation of OWL concepts to relational database in 2009. The classes in OWL ontology are mapped to tables in relational database, properties are map to relations and attributes and other ontological concepts like constraints are stored in special metadata table [15].

For implementation purpose they implemented the prototype tool as a plug-in for an ontology editor protégé. They choose an OWL file through user interface module of a tool. Ontology is presented graphically and connection is established with relational database server. Next step is validation of ontology. After ontology validation, OWL file is into Jena API. Its OWL to Relational database transformation module transforms OWL concepts to relational schema. Some parts of ontological information is not transformed like class complements, intersection and union class. Some property relations are also missing. Further extension in their method is required. [15].

Wei *et al.* discover simple mapping between OWL ontology to relational database but their approach is semi-automatic. They transform relational database and ontology into directed labeled graphs and reuse the schema matching tool named "COMA". They construct virtual documents for the entities in relational schema as well as ontology for semantic information. They also calculate confidence measures between virtual documents with the help of TF/IDF (information retrieval method) model. They discover simple mappings using the above calculation and then validate the consistency of mapping. They also create contextual mappings to specify the conditions of transformation. View-based mappings are created with the help of context match algorithm. They implemented their approach in java and named it "MARSON" (mapping between relational schemas and ontology). To evaluate MARSON, experiments are conducted to measure the performance of discovering simple mappings and then to measure the efficiency to create contextual mapping. Their approach is useful but requires machine learning techniques to get other useful semantic mappings [16].

Deise *et al.* provides a framework for storing XML files to relational database called "X2Rel" and "OntoRel". They generate ontology from XML documents with the help of "OntoGen" then transform OWL ontology to relational model and apply certain transformation rules. The drawback of their approach is that it transforms only main OWL constructs [17].

Ernestas *et al.* proposes hybrid approach to transform OWL ontology to relational database in 2011. Their transformation approach is based on common semantics of OWL and relational database. The ontology constructs which have no direct equivalence in database are stored in meta tables. For semantic preservation, they introduce certain requirements and according to them ontology transformation should fulfill certain "Normalization rules".

They give integrity rules for consistency of ontology. For implementation purpose they created vehicle ontology under these rules. They integrate their plug-in with protégé ontology editor. The method is fully automatic and transforms few OWL constructs into relational database [18].

Ernestas *et al.* presents another approach for reversible and lossless transformation between OWL ontology and relational database in 2010. The ontology classes, properties and instances are mapped to database tables with representing axioms. OWL restrictions are stored in meta tables. They define transformation in QVT (query/view/transformation) relational language. This language has the capability to define bi-directional transformation. But more research work is required to improve query capabilities [19].

2.9   Discussion

When discussing ontology to relational database transformation, we notice that there exists many approaches for OWL to relational database and inverse mapping but they face certain problems i.e. loss of structure, loss of data, manual and semi-automatic. They are limited and in many cases they just perform initial mappings i.e. tables to classes and columns to properties.

We have summarized some existing approaches in Table 2.1 along with their drawbacks. This discussion is based on twelve different approaches.

Approach	Procedure or Idea	Drawbacks
Rule based transformation[13]	Transformation is based on some set of rules that are applied to ontology.	Few constructs are lost during transformation (sub- properties), property restrictions.
OWL to ER and ER to OWL[3]	Transform ontology to conceptual model	Indirect transformations. Only main concepts are transformed.
Oracle Semantic data storage[10]	Predefined facts are stored in database tables and can be directly accessed using SQL queries.	Only OWL main constructs are handled.
Storing ontology includes fuzzy data types[11]	A schema structure can store ontology with fuzzy data types into database.	It covers only main constructs of OWL.
Large scale ontology management[12]	Ontological information is directly represented in relational database tables.	Relational structure is not preserved. Transformation is not fully automatic.
Transforming of Ontology Representation from OWL to Relational Database[14]	Propose an algorithm for mapping of ontology to relational database.	Only covers a part of OWL syntax
Mapping of OWL ontology concepts to RDB Schemas approach [15]	Use some principles and algorithm for automatic transformation.	But it lacks mappings i.e. class complements, intersection, union, and property relations.
Simple mapping between OWL ontology to relational database[16]	Discover simple mappings using some mathematical method	Requires machine learning techniques to get other useful semantic mappings.
Mapping OWL Ontologies To Relational schemas[17]	"OntoRel" tool implementation which provides a mechanism for transforming OWL ontology's to relational database.	The drawback of "OntoRel" is that it transforms only main OWL constructs and lack transformation for important ontological concepts
Reversible Lossless Transformation From OWL 2 Ontologies Into Relational Database[18]	A hybrid approach for reversible and lossless transformation between OWL ontology and relational database	Needed to improve query capabilities of the hybrid approach

Table 2.1 Comparison of existing approaches

Our study reveals that there exist many problems in direct transformation and mapping of ontology concepts to relational database. Some approaches claim that their method of transformation is fully automatic but the transformation process is incomplete and they miss important OWL constructs. Our research community needs to develop a tool from OWL ontology to relational database that is fully-automatic and can handle wider range of OWL constructs. This type of tool is required so that people can easily convert their ontology to the database. This tool will also help them in quick data searching and retrieval.

Chapter 3

Design

The importance of relational database in Semantic Web field is evident, so ontology to relational database mapping can be used in different applications or fields. Ontology can interoperate with a large amount of data that has already been stored in relational databases. Through mapping, we can share information. Querying the system will be more advanced, robust and optimized. A common goal is the consolidation of distributive information in the form of common vocabulary.

The building blocks in Web engineering are ontology and relational database. And large amount of Web data is stored in relational format. If relational schema and ontology were building independently, it complicates things. The majority of existing applications need integration among these systems. Through this mapping ontological data can be accessed from existing relational database applications.

Previous transformation approaches from OWL ontology to relational database, face certain problems i.e. loss of structure, loss of data, manual and semi-automatic. So our research focus is to develop a tool from OWL ontology to relational database that is fully-automatic and can solve above mentioned problems.

In this chapter, we describe our suggested approach and system architecture for ontology to database mapping. This chapter also contains mapping rules for transformation that are main focus of our research. A complete algorithm to transform ontology to relation database is described as well.

3.1 System Architecture

We propose an approach to automatic conversion of OWL ontology to relational database format. Figure 3.1, explains our approach for transforming ontology to relational database format.

- Initially, we choose an existing ontology file.
- Information is extracted about ontology constructs using Jena API.
- Build connection with SQL Server 2008 using "sqljdbc4" driver.

20

- After extracting this information, we transform ontological constructs into relational database format according to our defined mapping rules to ensure lossless transformation.
- Finally, a database is created.

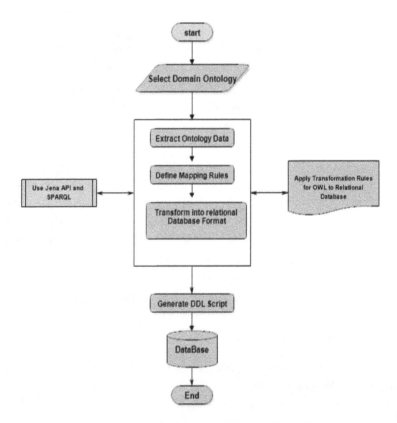

Figure 3.1   System Architecture for Ontology Transformation to Relational Database

Our main focus is to develop a tool for OWL ontology to relational database that is fully-automatic and can solve various problems in previous approaches.

3.2 Transformation Algorithm (Ontology to RDB)

We have developed an algorithm to map ontology constructs into relational database format. Following that algorithm the transformation process is given below.

1) First step is to choose any existing ontology. We are using Protégé ontology editor for this purpose.
2) The selected ontology or OWL file is first parsed to get Classes. Root class, super classes and subclasses are extracted by using Jena API.
3) Next step is to get OWL properties i.e. object type and data type properties. Data types of properties and restrictions are extracted as well.
4) Build database connection and transform extracted information into relational database format one by one.
5) Classes and subclasses are transformed into separate tables and one-to-one relationship is created among association classes according to mapping rules.
6) Single valued, functional and inverse functional object and data type properties are transformed as attributes of tables associated with corresponding class.
6) Multi valued properties and properties (both object and data type) having sub properties are transformed into separate tables.
7) Create separate metadata tables to store information about property restrictions.
8) Finally, ontology constructs are transformed into relational database.

3.3 Mapping Rules

We have identified multiple mapping rules to transform ontology to relational database. This section provides all the mapping rules used in transformation process. To briefly describe our mapping rules we have taken example ontology "Edu Ontology" which will be useful in understanding these rules.

According to these rules ontology classes are transformed into RDB tables and object type properties are transformed into column or table according to their relationship.

22

Ontology data type properties are transformed into columns or tables according to their values (single value or multi value).

3.3.1 Conversion of OWL Classes

Classes represent the basic concepts of domain ontology and they are the building block of different classification trees. These are used to group resources with same characteristics. Classes may be further divided into sub classes as shown in figure 3.2.

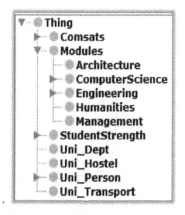

Figure 3.2 Classes and sub classes in "Edu ontology"

Rule 1: Each OWL Class (subclasses and association classes) will be transformed into a table in Relational database.

- Class name will become Table name.
- Table will be given a primary key.
- And a table that associates to a subclass is assigned a primary key and foreign key that reference to its "Super table" (one to one relationship between tables in relational database)

For example the classes in figure 3 Comsats, Modules, student strength and their subclasses will be converted into tables in relational database.

23

3.3.2 Conversion of OWL Properties And Their Data Types

Property describes various characteristics of class. They link two individuals and present relationship.

Object type Properties are relations between two individuals. And each object type property may have its corresponding inverse property. When we have defined object type property, we have to select relevant classes as domain and range of this property. Object properties have different types; they may be functional, symmetric, and transitive etc as shown in figure 3.3.

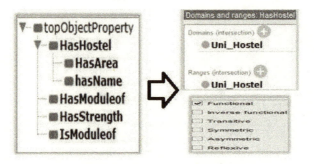

Figure 3.3 Object Type Properties

Rule 2: Single valued and functional object type property of OWL will be mapped into a foreign key in the domain table. This foreign key references a primary key in the range table.

- The name of the object property will become the name of foreign key.

The object type property "HasHostel" in figure 3.3 has domain and range class "Uni_Hostel". This property is functional property so it will be mapped into a foreign key in table "Uni_Hostel".

Rule 3: Single valued and inverse of object type property will be mapped into a foreign key in the table. This table will be related to the range of object property. This foreign key references the primary key in the domain table.

- The name of the inverse object property will become the name of foreign key.

Rule 4: If Object type properties are multi valued then they will be mapped into a separate table. This table will be assigned a primary key that's a combination of two foreign keys. One foreign key references the primary key of domain table and other references the range table.

- The name of the object property will become the name of Table by adding prefix "Obj_".

Rule 5: If object type properties are further divided into sub properties then they will be transformed into a table and their sub properties will be mapped into columns of that table.

- The name of the super property will become the name of table by adding prefix "Prop_".

In figure 4, the object type property "Has hostel" is further divided into sub properties. So this property will be transformed into a separate table in relational database.

Data types Properties describe relationships between individuals and data values (XML schema data type value). They also have domain and range. Domain class containing the property and Range has data type of this property as shown in figure3.4.

Figure 3.4 Data type property

25

Rule 6: Single-valued and Functional data type property will be mapped into a column in the domain table.

- The name of data type property will become the name of column.

In figure 5, "HasStudent" is single valued data type property so it will be mapped into a column in the domain table "StudentStrength" and its data type "int" will be converted into SQL data type (seen in table 2).

Rule 7: Multi-valued data type property will be mapped into a table and they will be assigned a primary key that is a combination of corresponding column and the foreign key that reference to the domain table of data type property.

- The name of data type property will become the name of Table by adding prefix "Data_".

Rule 8: If data type properties are further divided into sub properties then they will be transformed into a table and their sub properties will be mapped into columns of that table.

- The name of the super property will be the name of table by adding prefix "Prop_".

Rule 9: Data type conversion of data type properties is also handled.

We have converted data types of data type property from XSD to SQL, because OWL uses XSD data types. Table 3.1, shows how to convert different data types from XSD to SQL [2].

XSD data Types	SQL Data Types
Short	SMALLINT
Integer	INTEGER
negative Integer	INTEGER
nonnegative Integer	INTEGER
Unsigned Int	INTEGER
Integer	INTEGER
Negative Integer	INTEGER
nonnegative Integer	INTEGER
Unsigned Int	INTEGER
Long	INTEGER
Unsigned Long	INTEGER
Decimal	DECIMAL

26

Float	FLOAT
Double	DOUBLE PRECISION
String	CHARACTER VARYING
Normalized String	CHARACTER VARYING
Token	CHARACTER VARYING
Language	CHARACTER VARYING
NMTOKEN	CHARACTER VARYING
Name	CHARACTER VARYING
NC Name	CHARACTER VARYING
Time	TIME
Date	DATE
Datetime	TIMESTAMP
gYearMonth	DATE
gMonthDay	DATE
gDay	DATE
gMonth	DATE
Boolean	BIT
Byte	BIT VARYING
Unsigned Byte	BIT VARYING
hexBinary	CHARACTER VARYING
anyURI	CHARACTER VARYING

Table 3.1   Conversion of different data types from XSD to SQL

Table 3.1, shows how to convert different data types from XSD to SQL.

3.3.3 OWL Restrictions

To preserve all information about ontological constraints, we have stored this information in meta data tables. Every type of restriction has its own table.

"A property restriction is a special kind of class description. It describes a class having all individuals that satisfy the restriction. The value constraint "OWL: someValuesFrom" is a built-in OWL property that links a restriction class to a class description or a data range" [4].

Rule 10: "someValuesFrom" restriction maps to a table having multiple columns i) Restriction class (this column points to the table of the related restriction resource class),

ii) ON property (includes the property concerned), iii) domain class and iv) range class of property.

"The value constraint "OWL: allValuesFrom" is a property that joins a restriction class to either a class description or a data range. A restriction containing an "Owl:allValuesFrom" constraint is used to describe a class of all individuals for which all values of the property under consideration are either members of the class extension of the class description or are data values within the specified data range"[4].

Rule 11: "allValuesFrom" restriction maps to a table having multiple columns i) Restriction class (this column points to the table of the related restriction resource class), ii) ON property (includes the property concerned), iii) domain class and iv) range class of property.

"The value constraint "OWL: hasValue" is a built-in OWL property that links a restriction class to a value V, which can be either an individual or a data value. A restriction containing a "OWL: hasValue" constraint describes a class of all individuals for which the property concerned has at least one value semantically equal to V" [4].

Rule 12: "hasValue" restriction maps to table having columns, Restriction class (this column indicates the table of the related restriction source class), ON property (includes the property concerned), Domain class and Range class of property. In case of "Has value Restriction" Meta data table, a column "value" is added for storing the value of restricted resource of related property.

Rule 13: Inverse functional property will be mapped to unique constraint on the relevant column.

Chapter 4

Implementation

In this chapter, we will briefly describe all the software and languages used for the implementation of our transformation approach. To implement our proposed system for transforming OWL ontology to relational, we will use the following tools, languages and software.

- OWL
- Java
- Protégé
- Jena API
- SQL Server 2008

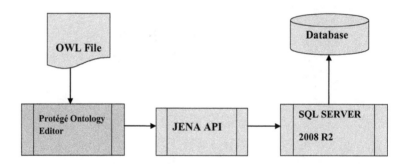

Figure 4.1 Transformation of OWL file into Relational database

Figure 4.1, presents the process of our transformation approach. We have selected some sample ontologies from standard protégé library. We have explored and manipulated these ontologies with the help of Protégé ontology editor. We have parsed these ontologies and have extracted OWL constructs with help of JENA API. Then we have applied defined mapping rules for transformation of ontology constructs into relational database. We have used SQL SERVER 2008 R2 as database engine. Finally, a database is created from the ontology that can be used for multiple purposes.

4.1   OWL

OWL provides three sub languages used for specific purpose. These are OWL-Lite, OWL-DL and OWL Full. The less expressive Sub-language is OWL-Lite. And OWL-Full is considered as high expressive sub-language. OWL-Lite is the simplest and easy sub-language. It is used in conditions where only a simple constraints and simple classification hierarchy are needed. OWL-DL is more expressive as compared to OWL-Lite while retaining computational completeness. OWL-DL and OWL-Lite are based on Description Logics. In OWL-DL, all OWL language concepts are included but can be used under some conditions. OWL-Full is the most expressive language. We have used OWL file as an input of our system. The system has utilized Protégé for OWL ontology management. OWL file is imported into Jena API. Jena API is used to parse OWL file and obtain constructs of OWL ontology.

4.2   Java Platform

We have implemented our system in java. We have used java platform "Eclipse" for our programming task. It becomes easy for developing and executing our tool with the help of Eclipse because it provides a complete and easy environment for java developers.

First, we have downloaded Jena API 2.5.4. After that we have added its jar files in Eclipse libraries. Then it needs to be added these jar files in source folder's build path. Jena API is used to extract ontology constructs.

We have used SQL server 2008 to save database after transformation process. We have downloaded "sqljdbc4" driver, which provides support to connect with SQL Server. We have added the Jar file of this driver in source folder's build path. To load the Jdbc driver, we have used the following command

Class.*forName* ("com.microsoft.sqlserver.jdbc.SQLServerDriver")

4.3 JENA API

JENA API is developed by HP laboratories. It is used to develop Semantic Web technologies with the help of following APIs. JENA provides a large number of tools and libraries to help us to build Semantic Web applications. It also provides libraries to handle RDF, OWL and SPARQL. Its rule-based inference engine provides support to perform reasoning based on different types of ontologies [8].

- RDF graph handling API

    An API used for reading, writing, and processing RDF data in XML, Turtle and N-triples format.
- OWL API

    Handle ontologies in OWL and RDF format.
- Inference Engine

    Used for reasoning with OWL and RDF data sources.
- SPARQL query engine

    It supports SPARQL query language through ARQ package.

We have used JENA 2.5.4. It is claimed that its libraries provide excellent support in modeling and parsing

4.4 SQL SERVER 2008 R2

It is a relational database management server developed by Microsoft. Its primary job is to store and manipulate data as requested by user or any other application. Its primary query language is SQL.SQL servers 2008 add some more features to SQL server like data management, Reporting Services and Integration Services [9].

It also contains a number of new facilities like

- Power Pivot for Excel
- SharePoint
- Master Data Services.

32

- Stream Insight.
- Report Builder 3.0....etc.

There are several advantages of a relational database over any other system i.e. solve data duplication, avoids inconsistent records, easier to change data, easier to change data format, data can be added and removed easily, easier to maintain security, gives scalability to the queries and reasoning on knowledge provided by ontology [9].

We have used SQL Server 2008 to save our information after transformation. First, the connection is built by using "sqljdbc4" driver. Then the extracted ontology constructs are automatically converted into relational database format.

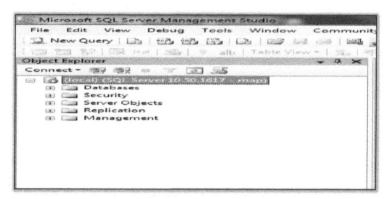

Figure 4.2 SQL Server 2008 R2

Figure 4.2, gives a brief view of SQL Server management studio.

4.5   Protégé

Protégé is an ontology editor and framework. It provides support in modeling ontologies. Protégé is based on Java language. It is expandable and provides a plug-and-play environment that helps in different application development. In protégé ontologies can be developed in different languages including OWL, XML schema and RDF(S). It is supported by large number of developers and various users. It is very helpful in understanding the ontological concepts. Brief Protégé documentation and tutorials are easily available on the Web.

We have used Protégé 4.2 to explore and manipulate different types of ontologies. We can view ontology in different forms with the help of Protégé ontology editor as shown in figure 4.3. It also provides reasoner to check the consistency of ontology. Protégé also support SPARQL query language for querying ontology [20].

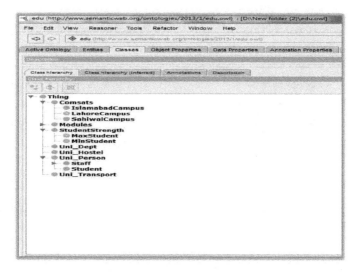

Figure 4.3 Protégé ontology editors

Chapter 5

Evaluation

In this chapter, we have presented a case-study to better explain the OWL to database transformation process. This case study shows that the proposed approach is automatic and effective.

5.1 Case Study

Different ontologies from multiple domains are presented to our system for transformation and numbers of experiments have been done. Experiments show that our proposed approach is fully automatic, effective and quick. The developed tool is easy to use. Our approach is lossless as well and performs the transformation successfully.

In this section, we have presented our automatic transformation process taking standard "Pizza Ontology" as an input. Pizza ontology has developed by Stanford university and popular to learn protégé OWL [21]. It has often been considered as important ontology for learning basic concepts of ontology and OWL language. We have chosen this ontology because pizzas are widely understood in all cultures or across the world. They are structural; pizzas are composed of base and have various toppings, color, size and weight. It is easy to build pizza ontology and understand the classification available in pizza ontology. The pizza ontology includes most of OWL features.

Pizza ontology consists of a large number of classes and subclasses. These ontology concepts are used to present main components of pizza domain, as illustrated in figure 5.3. This ontology has number of object type properties, data type properties and their sub properties, shown in figure 5.4 and 5.5. We have used Protégé ontology editor to explore and manipulate ontology. We have used our developed tool to transform pizza ontology into relational database format. The tool is developed with user friendly interface as shown in figure 5.1.

When we run this tool, it will ask the user to browse and select ontology. In the next step, user has to click "Transform into RDB" button, if the selected ontology is valid, transformation process starts and all the transformation rules are applied on ontology. A message will be displayed to the user that ontology is successfully transformed into database as shown in figure 5.2. Now, user can find a successfully converted database in SQL server.

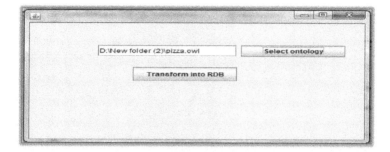

Figure 5.1 Tool Interface

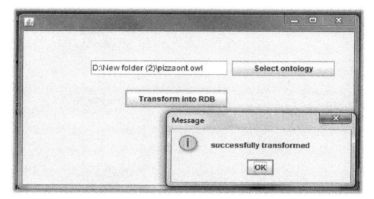

Figure 5.2 Transformation Completion

Below, we have described the transformation process taking "pizza" ontology as an input.

5.1.1   Step 1

After giving pizza ontology as input, next step is the extraction of ontological constructs e.g. classes, sub classes, object properties, data type properties, their domain and range, data types, restrictions etc with the help of Jena API. Later, above developed mapping rules are applied on the ontology.

37

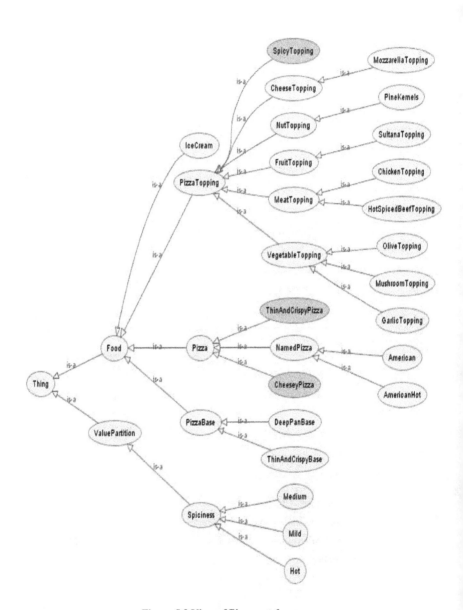

Figure 5.3 View of Pizza ontology.

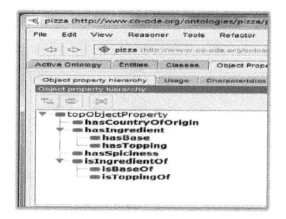

Figure 5.4 Object type properties in pizza ontology

Figure 5.5 Data type properties in pizza ontology

5.1.2   Step 2

According to rule 1, we transform all ontology classes into tables in RDB. Class name becomes table name and primary key is assigned as shown in figure 5.6. Table that relates to subclass is assigned a combination of primary key and foreign key that reference to its "Super table" (one to one relationship between tables in relational database) as shown in figure 5.7 and 5.8.

Figure 5.6 Conversions of ontology classes into tables into RDB

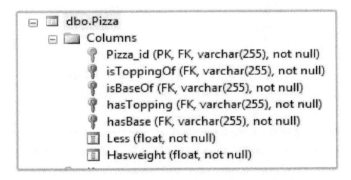

Figure 5.7 Conversion of ontology subclass into table in RDB

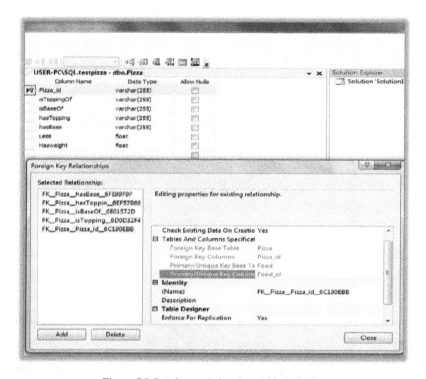

Figure 5.8 Ontology subclass into table in RDB

Figure 5.8, explains the one to one relationship between class and its related subclass. In Pizza ontology "Pizza class" is constructed as subclass of "food class". So when we have transformed pizza class into relational database format, a Pizza table is created with one to one relation to its super-class table Food. This mapping rule is applied in all association classes while transforming into relational database format.

5.1.3   Step 3

After mapping classes and subclasses into relational database format, we have transformed object type properties according to defined mapping rules. We have mapped single valued and functional object type property into foreign key in the table.

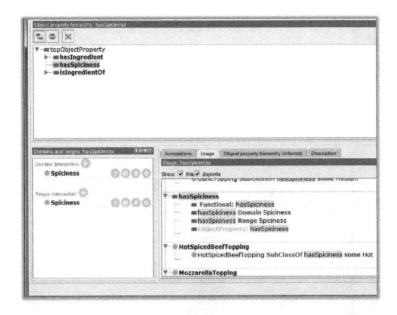

Figure 5.9 Single valued and functional object type property in Pizza ontology

In figure 5.9, "Has Spiciness" is functional property and has specified "Spiciness" class as domain and range of this property. This object type property maps to a foreign key in the table that relates to the class specified as the domain of the object property. This key reference the primary key in the table that relates to the class specified as the range of object property as shown in figure 5.10 and 5.11.

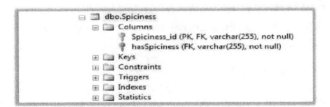

Figure 5.10 Transformation of single valued and functional object type property

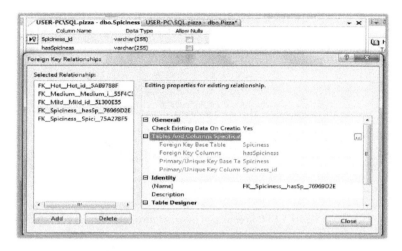

Figure 5.11 Transformation of single valued and functional object type property

We have transformed object type property that is "inverse functional" and single valued into a foreign key in the table that relates to range class of object type property. In figure 5.12, "is Base of" object type property is inverse of "has Base" object type property.

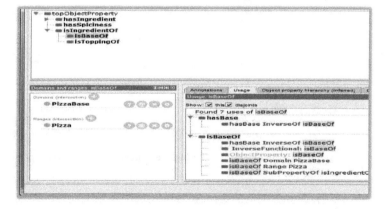

Figure 5.12 Inverse functional and single valued object type properties

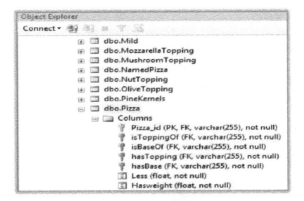

Figure 5.13 Conversion of inverse functional object type property

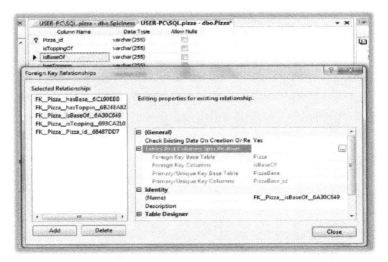

Figure 5.14 Conversion of inverse functional object type property

In figure 5.13 and 5.14, it can be seen that "Pizza" table has "isBaseOf" column. And it's a foreign key that relates to range class "PizzaBase"of object type property.

If object property named "has Ingredient" has two further sub- properties i.e. "has Base" and "has Topping" as shown in figure 5.15. After transformation, super-property "has ingredient" maps to a table in relational database and its sub properties maps to a column in corresponding table as shown in figure 5.16.

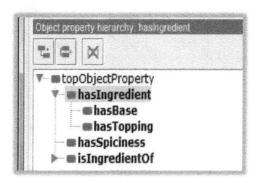

Figure 5.15 object type property "has ingredient" and its sub properties

Figure 5.16 Conversion of object type property that has sub properties

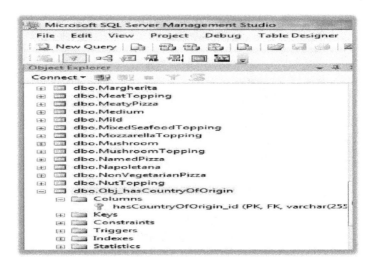

Figure 5.17 Conversion of Multi value object type property

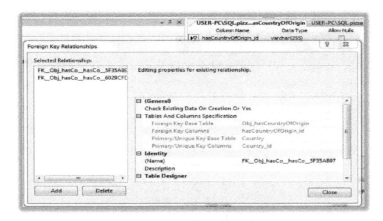

Figure 5.18 Conversion of Multi value object type property

Figure 5.17 and 5.18 explains that if Object type properties are multi valued then they will be mapped into a separate table. The object type property "hasCountryofOrigin" is multi valued property so it is transformed into table in database and is assigned a primary key that's a combination of two foreign keys. One foreign key references the primary key of domain table and other to range table.

5.1.4 Step 4

After mapping object type properties, data type properties and their data types are considered. If data type property is single valued e.g. in Pizza ontology "hasPrice" is a data type property and has specified "Pizza" class as its domain and has data type "float". This property maps to a column in the domain table as shown in figure 5.19. The column data type is the type specified as range of data type property converted from XSD to SQL data type (see table 1) as shown in figure 5.20.

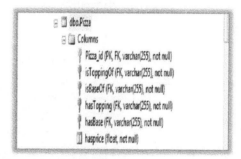

Figure 5.19 Conversion of single valued data type property

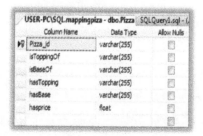

Figure 5.20 Conversion of single valued data type property and its data type (changes to float)

If data type property has sub properties e.g. in pizza ontology "has Weight" data type property has sub property "Less" as shown in figure 5.21. This property maps to a table in a relational database and its sub properties maps to a column the in corresponding table as shown in figure 5.22.

Figure 5.21 Data type property and its sub properties

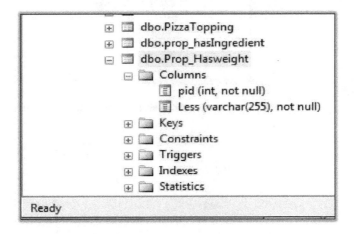

Figure 5.22 Conversion of data type property with sub- properties

5.1.5 Step 5

While converting OWL ontology into relational database format, we want to preserve all information of ontological constraints. For this purpose, we have stored this information in special meta data tables. Each type of restriction has its own table as explained before in the mapping rules.

Figure 5.23, explains "someValuesFrom" Restriction maps to a table having multiple columns i) Restriction class (this column points to the table of the related restriction resource class), ii) ON property (includes the property concerned), iii) domain class and iv) range class of property.

Figure 5.24, explains "allValuesFrom" Restriction maps to table having multiple columns i) restriction class (this column points to the table of the related restriction resource class), ii) ON property (includes the property concerned), iii) domain class and iv) range class of property.

In case of "hasValueRestriction" meta data table, a column "value" is added for storing the value of restricted resource of related property as explained in figure 5.25.

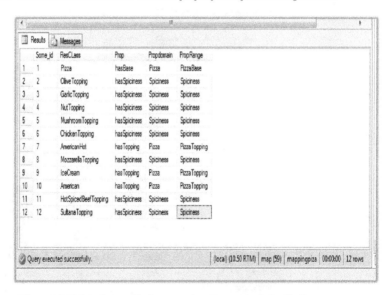

Figure 5.23 Meta data table "some values from restriction" after conversion

Figure 5.24 Meta data table "All_value_Res" after conversion

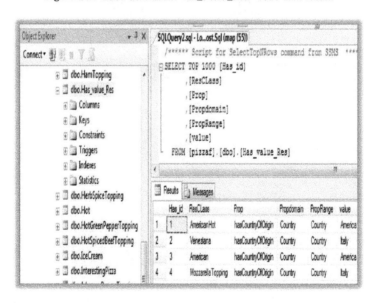

Figure 5.25 Meta data table "Has_value_Res" after conversion

5.2 Testing

To test the performance of our proposed tool, we have used 22 different ontologies. Most of them are downloaded from the standard Web site of Stanford University and remaining are collected from other sources. These ontologies have different sizes and they are from different domains. Testing of our tool with different types of ontologies increases its reliability.

In table 5.1, some necessary specifications of our machine used for testing are given.

Processor	CPU speed	OS	Memory	System type
Intel core i5	2.40GHz	Windows 7	4 GB	64 bit operating system

Table 5.1 Machine specifications

Table 5.2 gives detailed information about sample ontologies and their components. This information plays great role while testing of our approach. It becomes very easy to check the reliability of our tool by comparing this information to the final results.

We have applied our transformation approach on these sample ontologies. We have counted classes, sub-classes, properties etc. where it our approach is successful and not successful. These results are calculated manually. All the ontologies used were first manually converted into databases and then compared to the database created from our tool. In the same way the percentages are calculated e.g.

Number of Tables (Developed by our Tool) * 100

Number of Tables (Developed Manually)

Sample Ontology	Description	Number Of Classes	Object Type Properties	Data Type Properties	Restrictions
Pizza	About pizza and its components	>80	7	3	Yes
University	About university domain	29	6	2	Yes
Camera	About camera and its components	11	7	8	Yes
Trade	Define trade system	>70	20	3	No
Travel	Defines tourism	33	6	4	Yes
Event	About event handling	>60	7	10	No
Delegation	About management	18	5	3	Yes
Education	Defines education domain	36	12	>30	No
Car Advertising	About car advertising	10	3	8	No
Wine	About wine components	>15	3	1	Yes
Db1	About Library system	7	3	14	No
Docdb	About hospital	4	4	>10	No
Factorydb	About factory system	4	2	15	No
Vehicles	About Vehicles purchasing	6	6	>15	Null
Book storedb	About book publishing	8	7	>15	Null
Product-Sales	About inventory system	8	3	>15	Null
Atom-Primitive	About atoms of chemical elements.	>30	5	Null	Null
Bfo	Basic formal ontology	>30	Null	Null	Null
Igraph	About graph components	>30	>10	6	Null
Periodic table	About Periodic Table	>30	Null	Null	Null
Time-Individuals	About Time interval	7	8	Null	Null
Northwind	About inventory system	8	7	>20	Null

Table 5.2 Sample ontologies

Converted ontology concepts	Classes	Subclasses and their relation ship	Object properties	Data type properties and their data types	Restrictions
Pizza Ontology	94%	Yes, 40%	98%	Yes, all	Yes, converted to Metadata tables
Edu Ontology	100%	Yes, 60%	100%	Yes, all	Yes, converted to Metadata tables
Trade Ontology	100%	Yes, 60%	98%	Yes, all	Null
Travel Ontology	98%	Yes,60%	94%	Yes, all	Yes, converted to Metadata tables
Event Ontology	100%	Yes,60%	60%	60%	Null
Delegation Ontology	96%	Yes, 60%	100%	Yes, all	Yes, converted to Metadata tables
Education Ontology	100%	Yes, 60%	20%	70%	Null
Car Advertising Ontology	100%	Null	100%	Yes, all	Null
Wine Ontology	98%	Yes, 40%	100%	Yes, all	Yes, converted to Metadata tables
Camera Ontology	100%	Yes, 80%	100%	Yes, all	Yes, converted to Metadata tables
Db1 Ontology	60%	Null	100%	60%	Null
Docdb Ontology	100%	Null	40%	90%	Null
Factory Ontology	100%	Null	100%	90%	Null
Vehicles Ontology	60%	Null	50%	90%	Null
Bookstore DB Ontology	40%	Null	40%	50%	Null
Product-Sales Ontology	60%	100%	Null	70%	Null
North Wind Ontology	40%	Null	20%	70%	Null
Atom-Primitive Ontology	98%	Yes, 70%	100%	Null	Null

Bfo Ontology	100%	Yes, 60%	Null	Null	Null
Graph Ontology	100%	Yes, 40%	70%	20%	Null
Periodic Table Ontology	98%	Yes, 40%	Null	Null	Null
Time-Individual Ontology	98%	Null	90%	Null	Null

Table 5.3 Evaluation of our transformation tool

In table 5.3, we have given the final results after conversion of sample ontologies into relational database format. Table 5 shows that our tool is providing promising results.

Our transformation approach is based on "Mapping rules". Mapping rules have played an important role in lossless transformation of ontology into relational database format. In table 5.4, we have discussed the implementation and evaluation of defined mapping rules on some of ontologies.

Sample ontology	Rule 1	Rule 2	Rule 3	Rule 4	Rule 5	Rule 6	Rule 7	Rule 8	Rule 9	Rule 10	Rule 11	Rule 12	Rule 13
Pizza	✓	✓	✓	×	✓	✓	×	✓	✓	✓	×	×	✓
University	✓	✓	✓	×	✓	✓	×	✓	✓	✓	✓	✓	✓
Trade	✓	✓	✓	✓	✓	✓	×	✓	✓	×	×	×	✓
Travel	✓	✓	×	×	×	×	×	×	×	×	✓	✓	✓
Event	✓	✓	✓	×	✓	✓	×	✓	✓	×	×	×	✓
Delegation	✓	✓	✓	×	✓	✓	×	✓	✓	✓	✓	✓	✓
Education	✓	✓	✓	×	✓	✓	×	✓	✓	×	×	×	✓
Car adv	✓	✓	✓	×	✓	✓	×	✓	✓	×	×	×	✓

Wine		✓	✓	×	✓	✓	✓	✓	✓	✓	✓	✓	✓
	✓												
Camera	✓	✓	✓	×	✓	✓	×	✓	✓	✓	✓	✓	✓

Table 5.4 Implementation of mapping rules

Table 5.4 explains, most commonly used rules during ontology to database transformation. This can be helpful for future researchers to plan their research work in this domain.

We have also observed the time required for conversion from ontology to database by our tool. It is observed that conversion time is different for large and small ontologies. For large ontologies, it takes about 45 seconds and for small ontologies it takes only 15 seconds in transformation.

Chapter 6
Conclusion and Future Work

As the Semantic Web is gaining importance, there is a need of an efficient approach to map all ontology information into relational database so that it can be queried easily. One of the aims of Semantic Web is to make the Web work like database. Ontology plays an important role in Semantic Web and behaves like a foundation stone in a building. With the gaining popularity of ontologies, we need an efficient and automatic approach to transform all ontology constructs into relational database so that it can be queried easily. The mapping of ontology data into relational database ease operations like data searching and retrieval.

A lot of research work has been done on transformation of RDF/OWL concepts into relational database. But there exist problems in direct transformation and mapping of ontology to relational database. Most of transformation methods are semi-automatic and need human intervention. Some approaches claim that their method of transformation is fully automatic but the transformation process is incomplete and they lack handling important OWL constructs. Existing tools, plug-ins and utilities are not easily accessible and need improvement. In this thesis, we provide state of the art, approaches to transform ontology to database. We also discuss their drawbacks and benefits one by one.

We have proposed a fully-automatic transformation approach from OWL to database. Our transformation approach is loss-less and can map most of the constructs of ontology that were not handled before in any transformation approach. For lossless transformation of ontology constructs into relational format, we have created mapping algorithm and rules. We suggest that ontology classes will be transformed into tables, object type properties will be mapped into columns or tables, data type properties will be mapped into columns or tables according to mapping rules and restrictions will be store into meta data tables.

Due to this mapping approach ontological data can be accessed from existing relational database applications. This approach will play an important role in advance querying / query optimization.

Currently, our approach is capable to automatically transform most of ontology constructs into relational structure. In future, more research work is required to transform some other ontological information as class complement, comments, enumerated or intersection classes.

References

[1]   Grigoris. A, Frank. V. H. Semantic Web Primer. London: MIT press. (2003).

[2]   Irina, A., Ahto, K. and Nahum, K. (2007). Storing OWL Ontologies To Relational. *International Journal Of Electrical, Computer, And Systems Engineering* Vol. 1 No 4, Issn 1307-5179.

[3]   Syed, H.T, Juan, S. and Danial, M. (*2008*). Translating SQL Applications To The Semantic Web. *In Proceedings of the 19ᵗʰ International Conference on Database and Expert System Application (2008),* LNCS, Vol.5181, pp.450-464.

[4]   "OWL Web Ontology Language" at http://www.w3.org/TR/OWL-ref , accessed on 12-01-2013

[5]   "Database" at http://www.Webopedia.com/TERM/D/database.html, accessed on 12-01-2013

[6]   "Benefits of database" at https://www.sunadal.co.uk/db.php, accessed on 12-01-2013

[7]   "SPARQL Query Language for RDF" at http://www.w3.org/TR/rdf-sparql-query/, accessed on 18-01-2013.

[8]   "Jena Api" at http://jena.apache.org/, accessed on 18-01-2013.

[9]   "SQL Server 2008 R2" at http://sqlmag.com/sql-server-2008/sql-server-2008-r2, accessed on 18-01-2013.

[10]   Zhe, W. Karl R, George, E. Ankesh, K.and Vladimir, K. (*2008*). Implementing an Inference Engine for RDFS/OWL Constructs and User-Defined Rules in Oracle. *In Proceedings of IEEE 24ᵗʰ international Conference on Data Engineering, Mexico, Cancum.* pp. 1239-1248.

[11]   Carlos, D. Barranco. Jesus, R. Campana. Juan Miguel Medina and Olga Pons. (*2007*). On Storing Ontologies Including Fuzzy Data Types In Relational Databases. *Fuzzy System conference, IEEE International, July 23-26, 2007*, pp.1-6.

[12]   Richard, G. and Juhnyoung, L.(*2006*). Ontology Management for Large Scale Enterprise. *Electronic Commerce Research and Applications, spring*, Vol.5 (1), pp.2-15.

[13]   Gali, C. Chen, K. Claypool, and R. Uceda-Sosa.(2005). From ontology to relational databases. *Int. Workshop on Conceptual-Model Driven Web Information Integration and Mining (2005)*, Shanghai, China, Vol. 3289, pp. 278-289.

[14]   Ernestas,V. and Lina, N.E.(2006).Transforming Ontology Representation from OWL to Relational Database. *Information Technology and Control*, 35(3A), pp.333–343.

[15]   Ernestas,V. and Lina, N.E.(2009). Mapping Of OWL Ontology Concepts To RDB Schemas. *In proceedings of the 15th International Conference on Information and Software Technologies Kaunas, Lithuania, April 23-24, 2009*. ISSN 2029-0020, pp. 317-327.

[16]   Wei, H. and Yuzhong, Q. (*2007*). Discovering Simple Mappings Between Relational Database Schemas And Ontologies. *In Proceedings of the 6th international the Semantic Web and 2nd Asian conference on Asian Semantic Web conference*, pp. 225-238, ISBN: 3-540-76297-3 978-3-540-76297-3.

[17]   Deise, D.B.S., Tobias, D.C.A. and Eduardo, K.P. (*2011*). Mapping OWL Ontologies To Relational schemas. *In proceeding of Information Reuse and Integration (IRI), IEEE International Conference (2011)*.

[18]   Ernestas, V. and Lina, N.E. (2010).A Hybrid Approach for Relating OWL 2 Ontologies and Relational Databases. *Information Technology And Control*, ISSN 1865-1348, Volume 64, pp 86-101.

[19]   Ernestas, V. and Lina, N.E. (2011). Reversible Lossless Transformation From OWL 2 Ontologies Into Relational Database. *Information Technology And Control,* ISSN 1392 – 124X, Vol. 40, No.4.

[20]   "Protégé Ontology Editor and KnOWLedge Base Acquisition System" at http://protege.stanford.edu, accessed on 17-01-2013.

[21]   "Pizza ontology "at *protegewiki.stanford.edu/wiki/Pr4_UG_ex_Pizza*, accessed on 01-06-2013.

www.ingramcontent.com/pod-product-compliance
Lightning Source LLC
LaVergne TN
LVHW042345060326
832902LV00006B/395